Your Body and You

GROWING AND CHANGING

By Anita Ganeri

Illustrated by Vera Popova

PowerKiDS press

Published in 2025 by The Rosen Publishing Group, Inc.
2544 Clinton Street, Buffalo, NY 14224

Credits

Series editor: Julia Bird
Illustrator: Vera Popova
Packaged by: Collaborate

Note to parents and teachers: every effort has been made by the Publishers to ensure websites are suitable for children, that they are of the highest educational value, and that they contain no inappropriate or offensive material. However, because of the nature of the Internet, it is impossible to guarantee that the contents of these sites will not be altered. We strongly advise that Internet access is supervised by a responsible adult.

Cataloging-in-Publication Data

Names: Ganeri, Anita, 1961-, author. | Popova, Vera, illustrator.
Title: Growing and changing / by Anita Ganeri, illustrated by Vera Popova.
Description: Buffalo, NY : Powerkids Press, 2025. | Series: Your body and you |
Includes glossary and index.
Identifiers: ISBN 9781499445497 (pbk.) | ISBN 9781499445503 (library bound) |
ISBN 9781499445510 (ebook)
Subjects: LCSH: Child development--Juvenile literature. |
Children--Growth--Juvenile literature. | Maturation (Psychology)--Juvenile literature.
Classification: LCC HQ767.9 G326 2025 | DDC 305.231--dc23

Manufactured in the United States of America

CPSIA Compliance Information: Batch #CSPK25. For further information contact Rosen Publishing at 1-800-237-9932.

CONTENTS

GROWING UP

From the moment you're born, your body is changing. When you're a baby, you're small and can't do very much for yourself at first. Over time, you grow bigger and learn lots of new skills.

Sometimes, your body only changes a little bit. Sometimes, it changes a lot, very quickly. So, what happens to your body as you grow older?

You can find lots more about these changes in this book.

As you grow up ...

You learn how to walk and talk.

You learn how to ride a scooter or bike.

You learn how to look after yourself (well, most of the time anyway!).

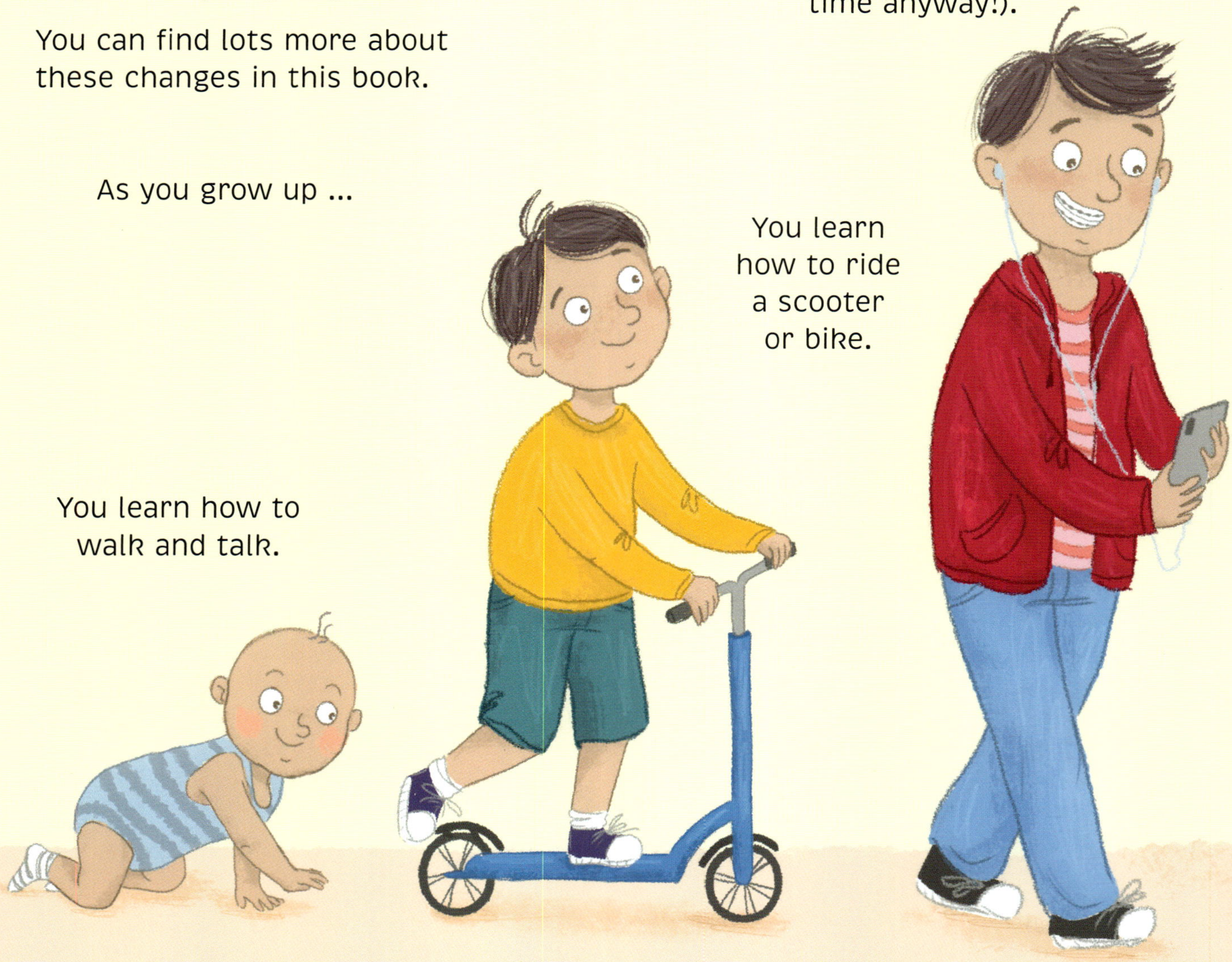

Some of the changes that happen to you are physical, like learning to walk or catch a ball. Some changes are about thoughts and feelings. Some are about the way you behave. All of these add up to make you the person that you are.

You learn how to look after others.

You learn what makes you happy and sad.

BECOMING A BABY

A baby grows inside its mother's tummy for nine months. This is when she is pregnant.

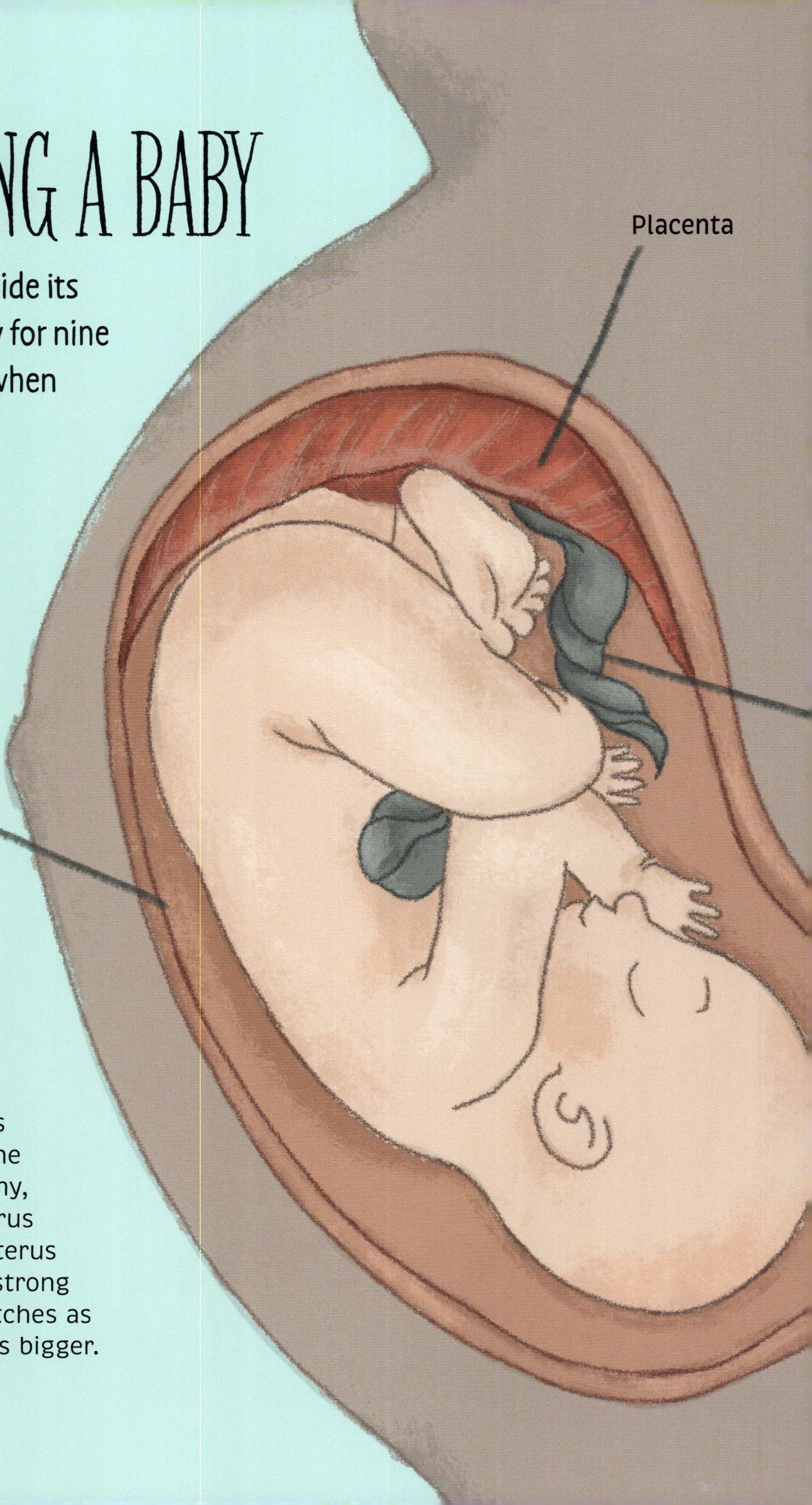

The baby grows inside part of the mother's tummy, called the uterus (womb). The uterus is made from strong muscle. It stretches as the baby grows bigger.

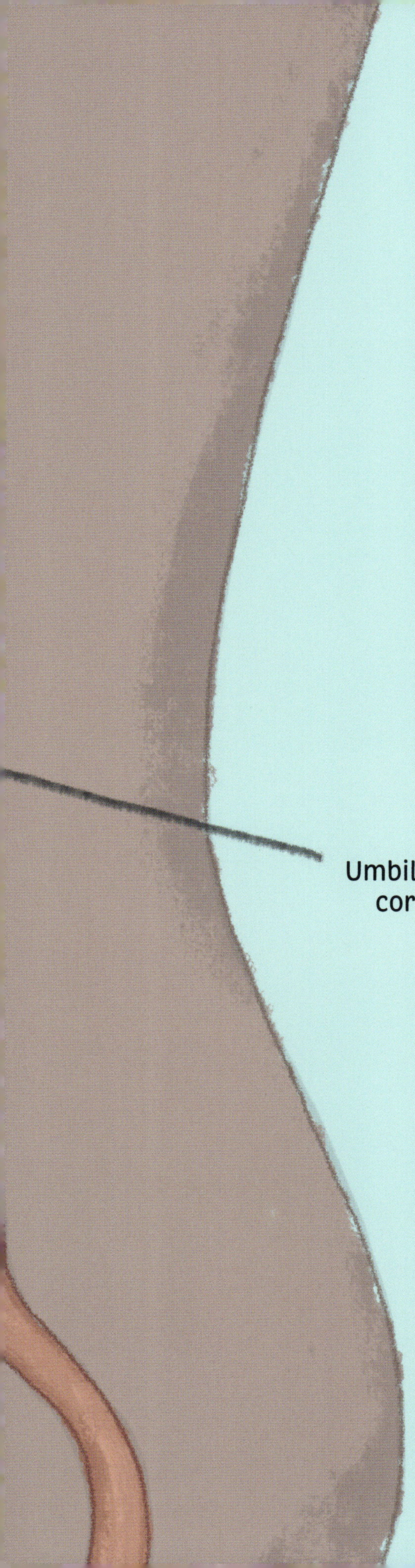

Inside its mother's body, the baby is safe from knocks and bumps. But it can't eat food or breathe air. It needs to get oxygen, food, and water from its mother.

Part of the uterus is called the placenta. It only grows when a woman is pregnant. A soft, bendy tube joins it to the baby. The tube is called the umbilical cord. Food and oxygen from the mother's blood pass across the placenta. They go through the umbilical cord into the baby's blood. The cord also takes away the baby's waste.

DID YOU KNOW?

When a baby is born, it can breathe on its own and drink milk. It doesn't need its umbilical cord anymore. The doctor cuts the cord. Your belly button shows where your umbilical cord used to be.

BEING BORN

After nine months inside its mother, the baby is ready to be born. The strong muscles in the uterus push it out of its mother's body.

The baby is usually born headfirst. Its skull has soft patches of skin in between the bones. These let its head change shape so it can squeeze out more easily.

A newborn baby's head looks huge compared to its body! This is because the baby's brain is already quite big. The baby needs a big brain because it has lots to learn. As you get older, the rest of your body grows and catches up to your head.

As a baby, you spend most of your time asleep. You can't talk, only cry! As you get stronger, you learn to sit, crawl, stand up, then take your first steps.

You also learn lots of new skills. By around a year old, you start to say a few words, like ma-ma and da-da.

FROM BABY TO TODDLER

As a newborn, you're about 20 inches (50 cm) tall. You grow fast! By one year old, you're almost twice as tall and three times as heavy.

Between the ages of one and three, you grow from a baby into a toddler. You change in some amazing ways. Here are just some of the things you learn to do.

Ages one to two

- ☆ Walk on your own
- ☆ Dance to music
- ☆ Build towers from blocks
- ☆ Scribble with a crayon
- ☆ Eat food with your fingers
- ☆ Say 50 to 100 words

Ages two to three

- ☆ Walk and run
- ☆ Throw and catch a ball
- ☆ Say 200 to 300 words
- ☆ Name things in pictures
- ☆ Drink through a straw
- ☆ Start getting dressed on your own

TODDLER TO CHILD

As you grow from a toddler to a child, you learn how to do many more things. You also learn how to play with other children and even make friends. By the age of four or five, you are ready to start going to school!

Ages three to four

- Ride a tricycle
- Use the toilet
- Stand on your tiptoes
- Speak in short sentences
- Know the names of colors
- Ask "Why?" all the time!

Ages four to five

- ☆ Sing a song
- ☆ Walk backwards
- ☆ Use scissors
- ☆ Say the alphabet
- ☆ Know the days of the week
- ☆ Get better at sharing

Ages five to six

- ☆ Tie shoelaces
- ☆ Ride a bike
- ☆ Play soccer and other games
- ☆ Begin to read and write
- ☆ Start school
- ☆ Make friends

DID YOU KNOW?

Your first teeth come through from around six months old until you are about three. When you are five or six, these teeth start falling out to make space for your adult teeth.

PUBERTY FOR GIRLS

Between the ages of eight and 13, a girl's body grows and changes a lot. It turns from a child's body into an adult's body. This is called puberty.

Your body changes on the inside and outside. These changes make it possible for you to have a baby one day, if you want to.

Puberty happens because of chemicals in your body. These are called hormones. They whiz around you in your blood. They get your body ready for being an adult.

Here are some of the main changes that happen to girls:

You might get some pimples.

Your breasts begin to grow.

Your sex organs grow inside you.

Your hips get wider.

DID YOU KNOW?

Most girls start puberty when they are about ten years old. But there's no set age. Don't worry if you start puberty earlier or later than that.

PUBERTY FOR BOYS

Boys go through puberty a bit later than girls, between the ages of around 11 and 15.

This is why girls are often taller than boys, even though they are the same age. Girls can also seem older and more grown up. But boys soon catch up!

Here are some of the main changes that happen to boys:

DID YOU KNOW?

You grow very fast during puberty, and your body changes shape. Your arms and legs get longer. Your hands and feet get bigger. Gradually, the rest of your body catches up.

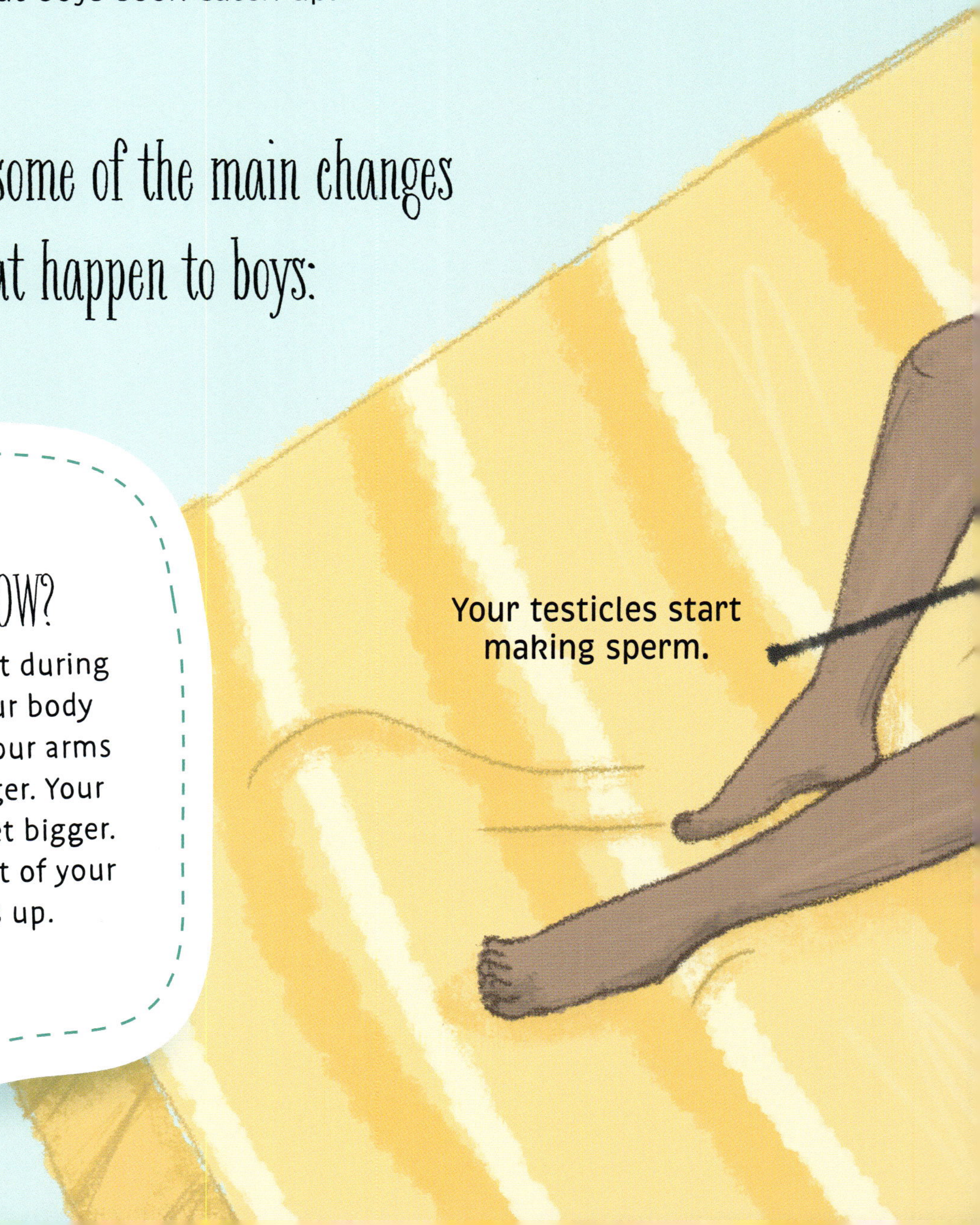

You might get some pimples.
Hair grows under your arms.
Your chest gets broader.
Hair grows on your face.
Your voice gets deeper.
Your muscles get bigger.
Your penis gets bigger.
You start growing pubic hair.

FUNNY FEELINGS

Puberty can sometimes feel scary and confusing. It's not just your body that's changing. It's also your feelings and moods.

You feel happy one minute, then sad the next. You get angry over the smallest thing. Your parents are driving you crazy. You wish everyone would just leave you ALONE.

Worse still, you have no idea why you're feeling like this.

Hormones cause these ups and downs. But you're also getting used to your new body, and the way you look. All of this uses up lots of energy. It's no wonder that you're tired and grumpy!

Don't worry, there's nothing wrong with you. It's all a normal part of growing up. Your hormones, and feelings, will settle down again.

DID YOU KNOW?

If you start getting angry, count to ten, slowly, until you feel calmer again. It will take time to learn to control your temper, but keep practicing.

TEENAGER TIME

When you reach the age of 13, you become a teenager. Being a teenager can be tricky, because you go through many more changes.

For a start, you're still growing. Sometimes, you grow very quickly; sometimes more slowly. By the age of 16, you are probably at your adult height.

But it's not just your body that's changing. You're also working out who you are, who your friends are, how you see the world, and where you fit in. You want to be treated as an adult and not as a child. But your parents keep telling you what to do. This can lead to arguments at home. The trouble is, you're not grown up yet. Your parents are trying to keep you happy and safe.

Friends become really important at this time. Some friendships last for a long time. Others change from week to week. You can also start liking boys or girls. You might get a funny feeling when you see them, and think about them all the time.

YOUNG ADULT

By your 18th birthday, your body usually stops growing. Your hormones settle down. You've gotten more used to all the changes. You are becoming an adult.

The front part of your brain is now almost fully developed. This is the part that helps you think ahead, make plans, and solve problems. You also get better at putting yourself in other people's shoes. You care more about others' feelings and the world around you.

This is also a time when there can be lots of changes in your life. You might have your first serious boyfriend or girlfriend. You might go to college. You might move out on your own. You might get a job. You probably have a better idea of who you are and what you makes you happy.

Sometimes, you still feel like a child. At other times, you feel like an adult. But you gradually learn the skills you need to make good choices. You settle into being grown up.

BEING GROWN UP

Being an adult brings lots of new experiences. You might get a good job, make a home of your own, and find a partner. You might have children of your own.

There are many kinds of families. Some have a mom and dad. Some have two moms or two dads. Some moms can't grow a baby inside them. They might adopt a child. This means becoming its forever family, when its first family can't look after it or keep it safe.

Think of all the families you know. What is your family like?

Having a job and taking care of a family can be tiring. Your body works hard being active, and you need to look after it.

Eating a healthy diet and doing exercise are the best ways of staying fit and strong. Exercise helps your heart and lungs to work well, and keeps you at a healthy weight.

GETTING OLDER

Your body changes again as you become older.

- ☆ Your skin become less stretchy, and you get wrinkles.
- ☆ Your hearing and eyesight become less sharp.
- ☆ You might find it harder to remember things.
- ☆ Your bones become weaker and break more easily.
- ☆ Your hair may get thinner and turn gray or white.
- ☆ Your reactions get slower.

Taking care of your body can help you to feel fit and strong for longer. It can also cut down the risk of getting many illnesses and diseases.

DID YOU KNOW?

The oldest person ever to have lived was Jeanne Calment from France. Born in 1875, she was 122 years old when she died in 1997.

Some older people stop working. They find they have more time than before to take up a new hobby or meet up with friends.

CHANGING TIMES

Find some photographs of you as a baby. Then find some of you as you are now. Have you changed? Can you still recognize it's you?

See if your grandparents, or an elderly friend or relative, can show you some photos of when they were young. How different do they look?

Throughout our lives, our bodies are growing and changing. Coping with these changes can be tricky. You can't wait to be a teenager. But you don't want to get old. You like becoming an adult and earning money. But you sometimes wish that you were a child again, without a care in the world.

These changes happen to everyone, and you will get used to them. Just remember, there are lots of things to do and enjoy at every stage of your life!

GLOSSARY

Oxygen
Gas in the air that we need to breathe to stay alive.

Partner
Someone you share your life with.

Penis
Part of a boy's sex organs.

Period
A few days of bleeding from a girl's body that happens about once a month.

Physical
Having to do with your body, rather than your mind.

Pregnant
When a woman is growing a baby inside her body.

Pubic hair
Short, wiry hair that grows around your sex organs on the outside of your body.

Reaction
Moving quickly when you need to.

Sex organs
Parts of your body that are used to make babies.

Sperm
Sex cells made inside a boy's body.

Testicles
Part of a boy's sex organs where sperm is produced.

Wrinkles
Lines on your face, when you get old.

FIND OUT MORE

Websites

kidshealth.org/en/kids/center/htbw-main-page.html

This website features fun, educational videos for kids.

https://www.ducksters.com/science/biology/humanbody.php

Learn more fascinating facts about the human body here.

kidshealth.org/en/kids/grow

This site features answers to many common questions about growing up.

Books

My Body's Changing: A Girl's Guide to Growing Up

Anita Ganeri, Franklin Watts, 2020

My Body's Changing: A Boy's Guide to Growing Up

Anita Ganeri, Franklin Watts, 2020

My Growing Body

C. J. Polin, PowerKids Press, 2023

INDEX